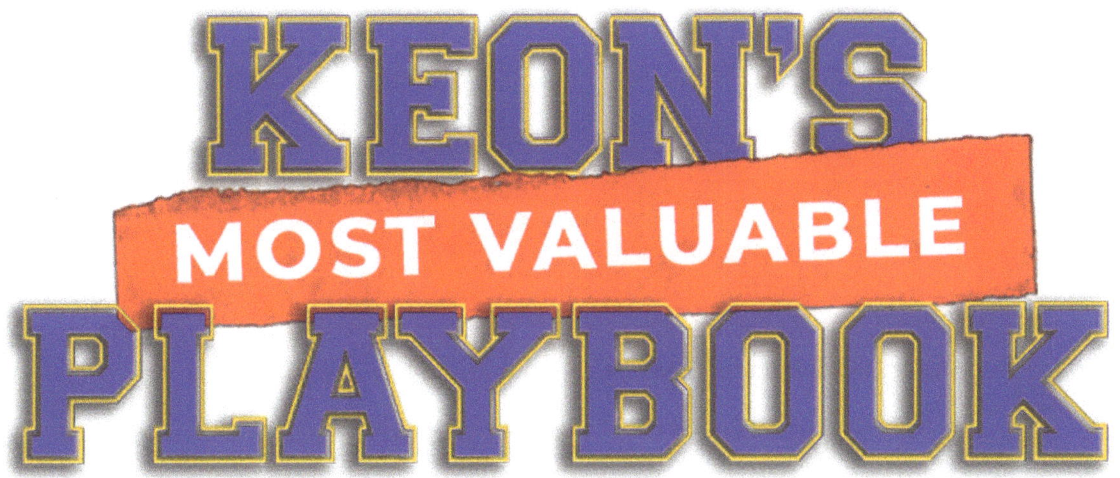

KEON COLEMAN AND SHARAÉ CELESTINE, PHD
ILLUSTRATED BY ASHINI I. SAMARATHUNGA

Keon Deante' Rashad Coleman was born on May 17, 2003, in Opelousas, LA. He played many sports throughout his childhood with the hope of becoming a professional athlete. "Keon's Most Valuable Playbook" is a story about a young boy dreaming big. Keon discovers his personal values through engaging with his support system and realizes these values will be the launching pad to his future success!

DEDICATION

This book is dedicated to Ravin Savoy. Ravin is the spark to so many flames. Many in her family and community can attest to how she pushes them to move towards their purpose despite obstacles. Ravin is a living testimony.

The MVP award goes to…

KEON COLEMAN!

MVP! MVP! MVP!

The crowd goes wild as I carry the huge golden trophy after leading my team to victory.

MVP! MVP! MVP!

I can only imagine what I would look like if my biggest sports dream would come true.

"Keon, your oatmeal is getting cold!"

I snapped out of my daydream and yelled,
"I'm coming, Momma!"

I quickly put on my shoes and hurried off to the breakfast table.

"Momma, I don't know how, but one day I am going to be an MVP."

"I believe you son." Momma responded. *"Come up with a plan and write it down."*

"Hmmm, I'll grab a notebook and a pen so I can get started!"

"Ok, Ke! I look forward to hearing about your plan at the end of the day, but right now I need all of my kids to focus on school and making good grades," Momma said.

I grabbed my notebook and booksack and rushed off to school, determined to figure out how to become an MVP.

*"**Wait up!**"* I yelled to my siblings.

It was quiz bowl day at school and the topic was local sports superstars. I did not want to be late to Ms. Hicks's class.

"Who knows a NFL player from Opelousas, LA?" asked Ms. Hicks.

Excitedly, I raised my hand, "ME! ME! ME!"

"Yes Keon," said Ms. Hicks.

"Devery Henderson," I answered.

"Good job, Keon!" Ms. Hicks responded.

"Yep, I'm going to the big leagues too. I'm working on a plan to be the MVP. What do you think should be a part of my plan?"

"I think you're off to a great start Keon, asking questions to learn is a key characteristic of an MVP," Ms. Hicks responded.

Hmmm, Ms. Hicks may be on to something.

I thought long and hard about what my teacher said. If I wanted to be a star, I should ask the stars in my life for some tips.

I quickly wrote my first entry in my notebook:

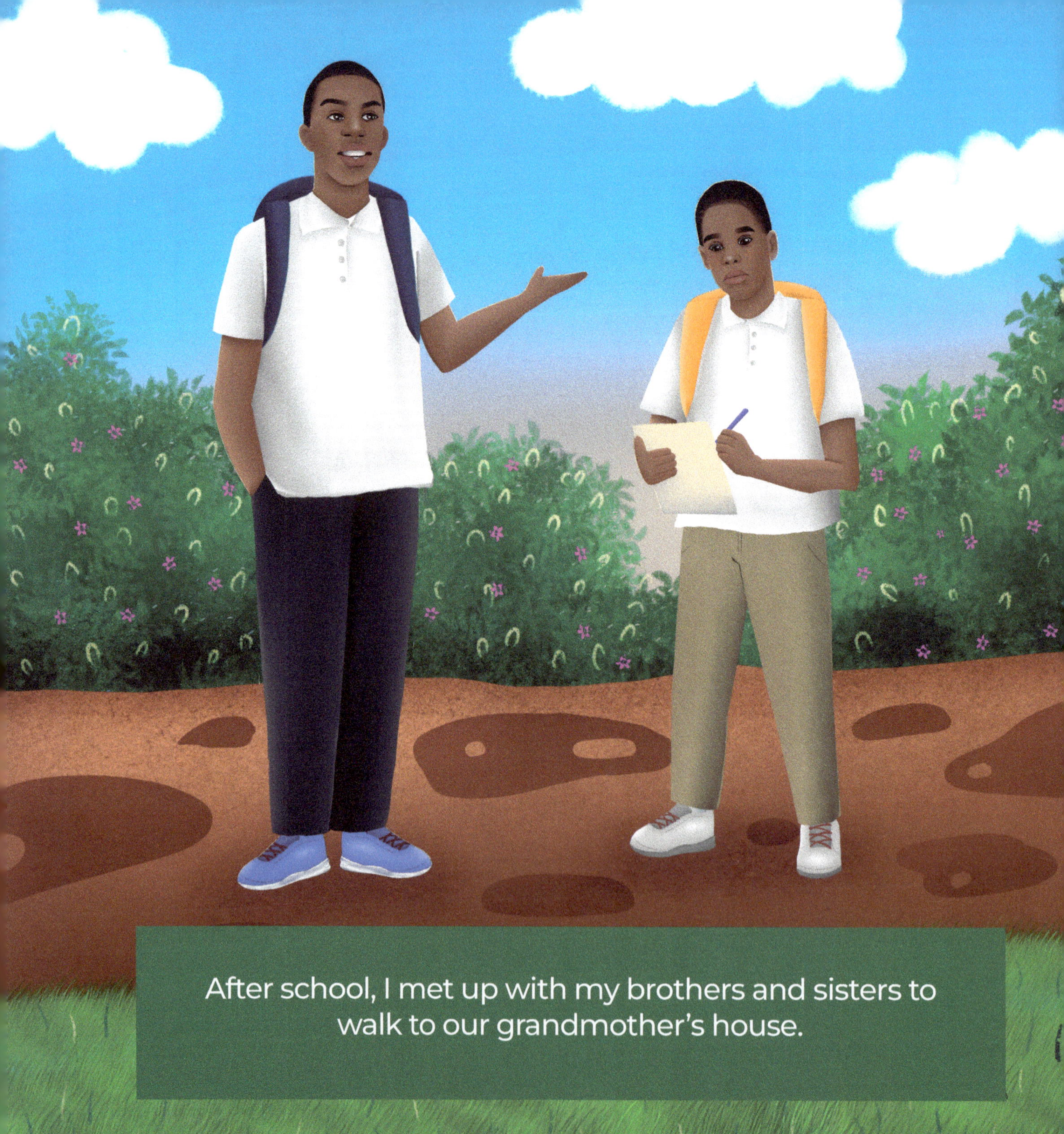

After school, I met up with my brothers and sisters to walk to our grandmother's house.

I decided I would ask my big brother Kaylan
what he thought.

Kaylan told me that I needed to be disciplined.
*"MVPs wake up early! They lift weights, stretch, and
run every day to get really fast."*

That's a lot, I thought to myself.

"Kaylan, will you help me?" I asked.

*"Yeah, Keon, I'll be your personal trainer. You have to
be ready to work hard,"* said Kaylan.

"Yes!" I shouted.

Then, I wrote in my notebook:

When we got to my grandmother's house,
I decided to ask her.

"MoMo Paula, I'm going to be an MVP one day. What
do you think should be a part of my plan to get there?"

"Eat your vegetables, mind your manners, and remember to put God first and pray," she said.

"Will you cook something healthy for me?" I asked.

"Yeah, I'll cook," said MoMo Paula.

"Great!"

I wrote down MoMo Paula's advice:

#3 MVPS eat healthy food, mind their manners, put God first, and say their prayers.

I grabbed my snack from the table at MoMo Paula's house and headed to practice. I knew Coach Randy would give me a good tip.

"Coach Randy, I'm making a plan to become an MVP and I want to know what you think I should add?"

"Be a helper and good teammate,"
Coach Randy replied.

"Will you show me how?" I asked.

Coach Randy said, *"I sure will!"*

For the rest of the season, Coach Randy taught
me how to work with my teammates to score
points and win games.

He reminded me that no one wants to see one superstar,
they want to see a team of superstars.

This was definitely going into the plan.

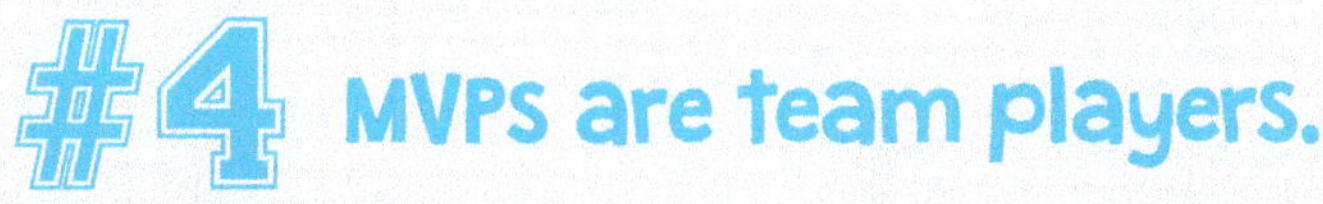

When practice was over, I was so excited to see my Momma. I threw my gear in the trunk and jumped in the backseat eager to share my plan!

"How was your day, Keon?" asked Momma.

"It was amazing! I have a plan to become an MVP!"

"Let's hear it," said Momma.

"I will ask questions to the superstars in my life. I will be disciplined, so I'm going to wake up early every morning, go for a run, and lift weights. I will put God first, say my prayers, mind my manners, and eat healthy food. Most importantly, I'm going to be a good teammate. I even have people who are going to help me get there!"

"That's great, Keon! I'm proud of you for looking to your village for help with creating your plan. Always remember to be on your best behavior, make good grades, and keep good company," Momma added.

"Oh yeah, let me write that down!" My final tip:

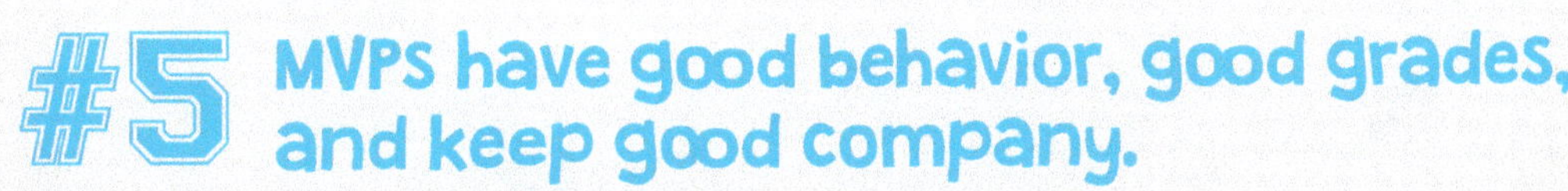

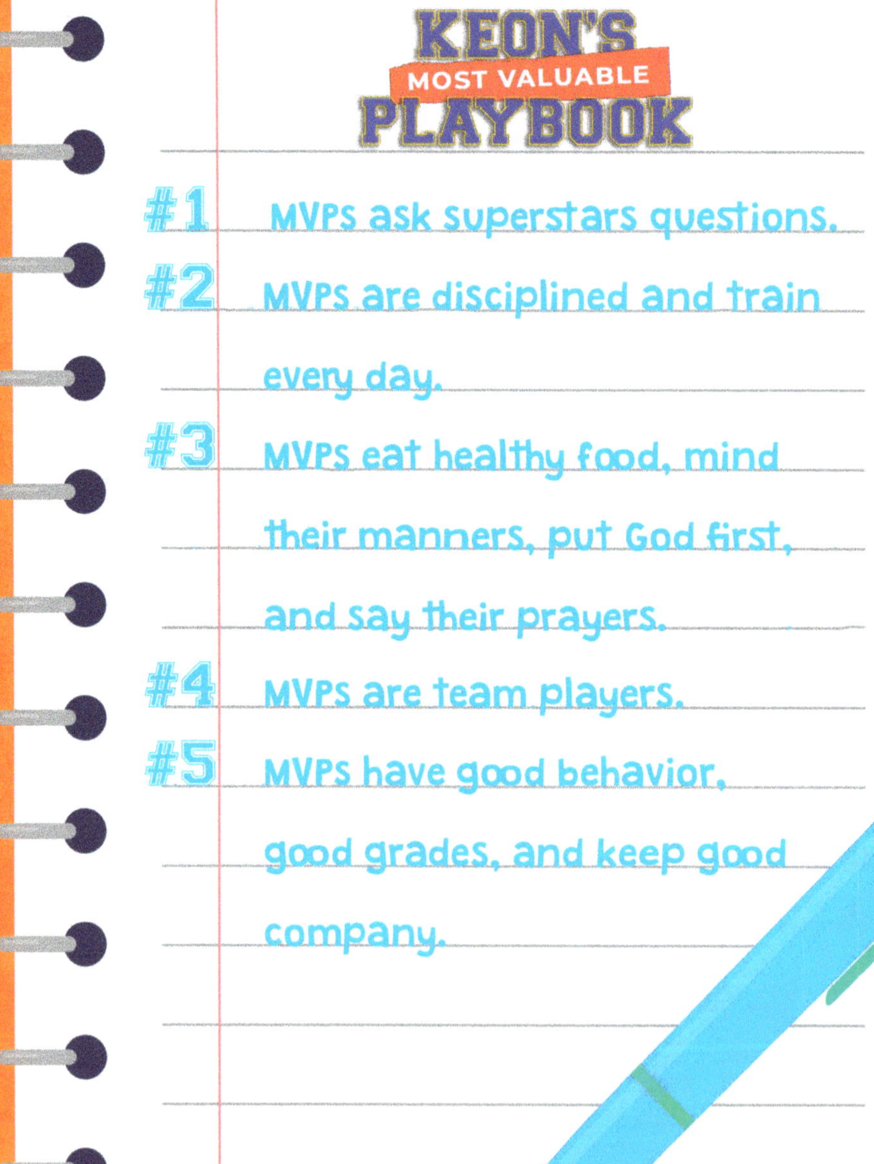

KEON'S
MOST VALUABLE
PLAYBOOK

#1 MVPs ask superstars questions.
#2 MVPs are disciplined and train every day.
#3 MVPs eat healthy food, mind their manners, put God first, and say their prayers.
#4 MVPs are team players.
#5 MVPs have good behavior, good grades, and keep good company.

Momma asked, *"What are you going to name this plan, Keon?"*

I thought for a second.

I flipped my notebook to the front cover and wrote in big letters across the front:

KEON'S MOST VALUABLE PLAYBOOK.

LECOM
NFL
Lion

KEON'S SPORTS TIMELINE

CHILD

OPELOUSAS LITTLE LEAGUE
Baseball (Ages 5 - 12)
Football (Ages 5 - 12)

OPELOUSAS BIDDY BASKETBALL (Ages 5 - 12)

PRE-TEEN/TEEN

OPELOUSAS CATHOLIC HIGH SCHOOL
Basketball (Ages 13 - 17)
Football (Ages 13 - 17)
Track (Ages 15 - 17)

AAU
Opelousas Rockets AAU Basketball (Ages 10-17)
LivOn AAU Basketball (Ages 15-17)

COLLEGE

MICHIGAN STATE
Basketball (Age 18)
Football (Ages 18 - 19)

FLORIDA STATE
Football (Age 20)

PRO

NATIONAL FOOTBALL LEAGUE
33rd Draft Pick to the Buffalo Bills (Age 21)

Hey Dreamer,

I hope my story inspires you to dream big and when you accomplish your dream - dream again. Just wanted to write you a letter and drop a few gems for you to remember. Check them out!

1. There will be times that school is hard. Ask questions, take breaks, but never give up.

2. There will be times when you want to hang out. Choose the friends that have the same goals as you.

3. There will be times that you may not do everything the right way or the way your parents told you to. Take "your lick" (accountability) and do better next time.

4. There will be times that you are unsure if you are going to be successful. Stay focused and disciplined.

5. There will be times that you are the best player on the team. Help your teammates.

6. There will be times that you are not the best player on the team. Study the game and learn from the best.

7. There will be things you are naturally good at doing and some things will be tough to do. Work hard at developing the skills that do not come naturally.

8. Never stop having fun!

My grandmother always told me that "even if things don't look good in the natural, it is good in the spiritual". What she meant was even if things do not look like they are going to work out the way you want, do not stop believing because eventually it will happen.

Remember to write down your dreams and repeat them out loud often to remind yourself that they will one day come to pass. My go to scripture is Habakkuk 2:2, write the vision and make it plain so he who reads it will run to it and even though it may tarry wait for it for surely it will come at an appointed time.

The following worksheets will help get you started on your Dream Journey. I believe in you!

YOUR NUMBER ONE FAN,

Keon

....

(Your Name)

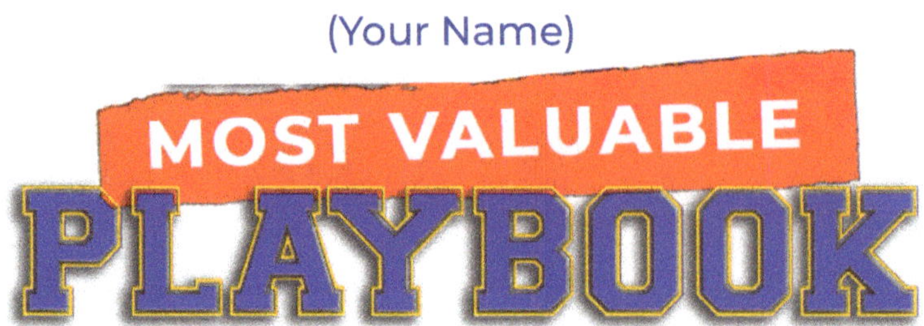

What is your dream?

____

____

____

____

____

____

____

____

____

____

Who are the superstars in your life that can help you reach your dream?

What advice have the stars in your life given you to help you accomplish your goal?

1.____

____

____

2.____

____

____

3.____

____

____

4.____

____

____

5.____

____

____

Think about your biggest dreams coming true. What do you see when you look in the mirror? Draw a picture below.

ABOUT THE CO-AUTHOR

Sharaé Celestine, PhD

Sharae Celestine was born and raised in Opelousas, LA. She currently resides in Houston, TX. Sharae has earned her PhD in Leadership Studies, in which her focus specializes in empowering others to develop their Emotional Intelligence. She enjoys volunteering with children and this is Sharae's first literary work. Her hope is that this book will inspire the reader that no dream is too big when you have the right support, a plan, and determination!

Ashini I. Samarathunga

Ashini Samarathunga is a passionate children's book illustrator with over seven years of experience. Her love for cartoons shines through her vibrant and engaging illustrations. Whether it's bringing characters to life or creating captivating book covers, Ashini loves to spark imaginations and create unforgettable adventures for young readers.